This Book Belongs to:

_____

STUDENT Spotlight

DATE: _____

It made me smile today when one of my
students said...

"

_____

_____

_____

_____

"

_____

A student who stood out was...

_____

_____

_____

_____

_____

A student that inspired me was...

_____

_____

_____

_____

_____

Who was struggling? Why?

_____

_____

_____

_____

A student made me laugh when...

_____

_____

_____

_____

WEEKLY *goals*

WEEK OF: _____

- _____
- _____
- _____
- _____
- _____
- _____
- _____
- _____
- _____

Things to note: _____

_____

A good teacher is like a candle -
it consumes itself to light the way
for others. **– MUSTAFA KEMEL**

Lesson plan topics

Teachers should be full of ideas instead of stuffed with facts.
- AUTHOR UNKNOWN

Use this space to doodle,
brainstorm, journal or take notes
free your mind

Something I want to focus on as a teacher is...

_____

_____

_____

_____

_____

How did you make learning fun for your students this week:

- _____

- _____

- _____

- _____

- _____

TEACHING
reflections

Reflecting on your day including the highs and lows
is a great way to learn from your experiences

DATE: _____

What were the highlights of your day?

_____

_____

_____

_____

_____

_____

_____

_____

_____

What would you have done
differently today?

_____

_____

_____

_____

_____

_____

_____

What are three things you will try in the
coming days to help your students succeed?

DATE: _____

What is your favorite part of being a teacher?

_____

_____

_____

_____

What was your biggest motivation today?

_____

_____

_____

_____

What was your biggest challenge today?

_____

_____

_____

_____

IT TAKES A BIG *heart* TO TEACH LITTLE *minds*

What are some successes you have seen lately?

What areas of growth have you seen professionally? Personally?

DATE: _____

What topics are you most looking forward to teaching?

What topic have you been enjoying teaching lately?

_____

_____

_____

_____

_____

What topics are any of your students struggling with?
How can you help them?

_____

_____

_____

_____

_____

_____

List four things you are proud of accomplishing with
your students recently?

Notes

STUDENT Spotlight

DATE: _____

It made me smile today when one of my
students said...

"

_____

_____

_____

_____

"

_____

A student who stood out was...

_____

_____

_____

_____

A student that inspired me was...

_____

_____

_____

_____

_____

Who was struggling? Why?

_____

_____

_____

_____

A student made me laugh when...

_____

_____

_____

_____

WEEKLY *goals*

WEEK OF: _____

- _____
- _____
- _____
- _____
- _____
- _____
- _____
- _____
- _____

Things to note: _____

_____

Teaching kids to count is fine, but teaching them what counts is best.
- BOB TALBERT

Lesson plan topics

Tell me and I forget. Teach me and I remember. Involve
me and I learn.
– BENJAMIN FRANKLIN

Use this space to doodle,
brainstorm, journal or take notes
free your mind

Something I want to focus on as a teacher is...

_____

_____

_____

_____

_____

_____

How did you make learning fun for your students this week:

- _____

- _____

- _____

- _____

- _____

TEACHING
reflections

Reflecting on your day including the highs and lows
is a great way to learn from your experiences

DATE: _____

What were the highlights of your day?

_____

_____

_____

_____

_____

_____

_____

_____

_____

What would you have done differently today?

_____

_____

_____

_____

_____

_____

_____

_____

What are three things you will try in the coming days to help your students succeed?

DATE: _____

What is your favorite part of being a teacher?

_____

_____

_____

_____

What was your biggest motivation today?

_____

_____

_____

_____

What was your biggest challenge today?

_____

_____

_____

_____

IT TAKES A BIG *heart* TO TEACH LITTLE *minds*

What are some successes you have seen lately?

What areas of growth have you seen professionally? Personally?

DATE: _____

What topics are you most looking forward to teaching?

What topic have you been enjoying teaching lately?

_____

_____

_____

_____

_____

What topics are any of your students struggling with?
How can you help them?

_____

_____

_____

_____

_____

_____

List four things you are proud of accomplishing with
your students recently?

Notes

STUDENT Spotlight

DATE: _____

It made me smile today when one of my
students said...

"

_____

_____

_____

_____

"

_____

A student who stood out was...

_____

_____

_____

_____

_____

A student that inspired me was...

_____

_____

_____

_____

Who was struggling? Why?

_____

_____

_____

A student made me laugh when...

_____

_____

_____

_____

WEEKLY *goals*

WEEK OF: _____

- _____
- _____
- _____
- _____
- _____
- _____
- _____
- _____

Things to note: _____

_____

Nine-tenths of education is encouragement.
- ANATOLE FRANCE

Lesson plan topics

I am not a teacher, but an awakener.
- ROBERT FROST

Use this space to doodle,
brainstorm, journal or take notes

free your mind

Something I want to focus on as a teacher is...

_____

_____

_____

_____

_____

How did you make learning fun for your
students this week:

- _____

- _____

- _____

- _____

- _____

TEACHING
reflections

Reflecting on your day including the highs and lows
is a great way to learn from your experiences

DATE: _____

What were the highlights of your day?

_____

_____

_____

_____

_____

_____

_____

_____

_____

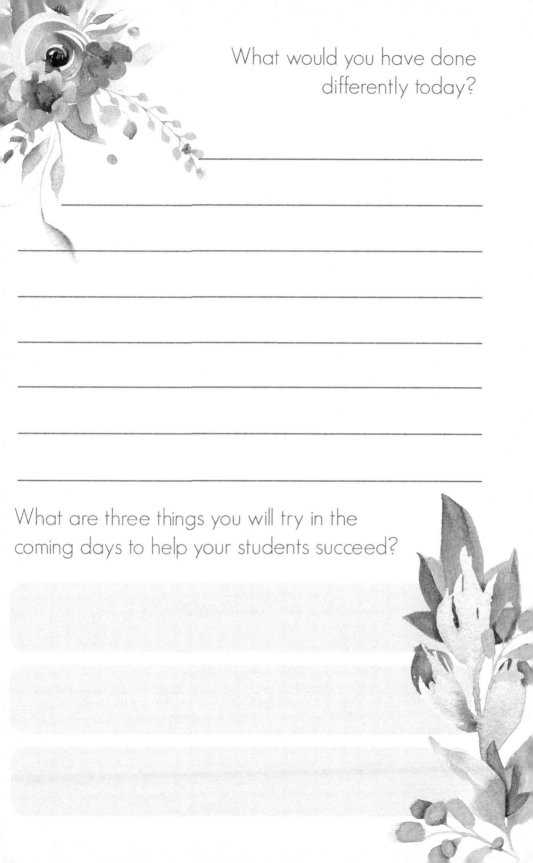

What would you have done
differently today?

_____

_____

_____

_____

_____

_____

_____

_____

What are three things you will try in the
coming days to help your students succeed?

DATE: _____

What is your favorite part of being a teacher?

_____

_____

_____

_____

What was your biggest motivation today?

_____

_____

_____

What was your biggest challenge today?

_____

_____

_____

_____

IT TAKES A BIG *heart* TO TEACH LITTLE *minds*

What are some successes you have seen lately?

What areas of growth have you seen professionally? Personally?

DATE: _____

What topics are you most looking forward to teaching?

What topic have you been enjoying teaching lately?

_____

_____

_____

_____

_____

_____

What topics are any of your students struggling with? How can you help them?

_____

_____

_____

_____

_____

List four things you are proud of accomplishing with your students recently?

Notes

STUDENT Spotlight

DATE: _____

It made me smile today when one of my
students said...

"

_____

_____

_____

_____

"

_____

A student who stood out was...

_____

_____

_____

_____

_____

A student that inspired me was...

_____

_____

_____

_____

_____

Who was struggling? Why?

_____

_____

_____

_____

A student made me laugh when...

_____

_____

_____

_____

WEEKLY *goals*

WEEK OF: _____

- _____
  _____
- _____
  _____
- _____
  _____
- _____
  _____
- _____
  _____
- _____
  _____
- _____
  _____
- _____
  _____
- _____
  _____

Things to note: _____

_____

The art of teaching is the art of assisting discovery.
- MARK VAN DOREN

Lesson plan topics

A teacher affects eternity; he can never tell where his influence stops.
- HENRY B. ADAMS

Use this space to doodle,
brainstorm, journal or take notes

free your mind

Something I want to focus on as a teacher is...

_____

_____

_____

_____

_____

How did you make learning fun for your students this week:

- _____

- _____

- _____

- _____

- _____

TEACHING *reflections*

Reflecting on your day including the highs and lows is a great way to learn from your experiences

DATE: _____

What were the highlights of your day?

_____

_____

_____

_____

_____

_____

_____

_____

_____

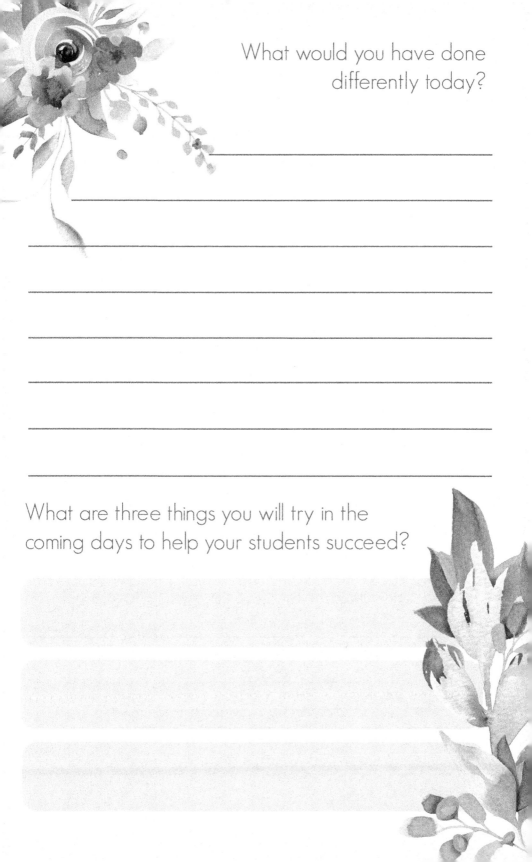

What would you have done
differently today?

_____

_____

_____

_____

_____

_____

_____

_____

What are three things you will try in the
coming days to help your students succeed?

DATE: _____

What is your favorite part of being a teacher?

_____

_____

_____

_____

What was your biggest motivation today?

_____

_____

_____

_____

What was your biggest challenge today?

_____

_____

_____

_____

IT TAKES A BIG *heart* TO TEACH LITTLE *minds*

What are some successes you have seen lately?

What areas of growth have you seen professionally? Personally?

DATE: _____

What topics are you most looking forward to teaching?

What topic have you been enjoying teaching lately?

_____

_____

_____

_____

_____

What topics are any of your students struggling with?
How can you help them?

_____

_____

_____

_____

_____

_____

List four things you are proud of accomplishing with
your students recently?

Notes

STUDENT *Spotlight*

DATE: _____

It made me smile today when one of my
students said...

"

_____

_____

_____

_____

"

_____

A student who stood out was...

_____

_____

_____

_____

_____

A student that inspired me was...

_____

_____

_____

_____

_____

Who was struggling? Why?

_____

_____

_____

_____

A student made me laugh when...

_____

_____

_____

_____

WEEKLY *goals*

WEEK OF: _____

- ● _____
- ● _____
- ● _____
- ● _____
- ● _____
- ● _____
- ● _____
- ● _____
- ● _____

Things to note: _____

_____

To teach is to learn twice over.
- JOSEPH JOUBERT

Lesson plan topics

Education is not the filling of a pail,
but the lighting of a fire.
- WILLIAM BUTLER YATES

Use this space to doodle,
brainstorm, journal or take notes

free your mind

Something I want to focus on as a teacher is...

_____

_____

_____

_____

_____

_____

How did you make learning fun for your
students this week:

- _____

- _____

- _____

- _____

- _____

TEACHING
reflections

Reflecting on your day including the highs and lows
is a great way to learn from your experiences

DATE: _____

What were the highlights of your day?

_____

_____

_____

_____

_____

_____

_____

_____

_____

What would you have done differently today?

_____

_____

_____

_____

_____

_____

_____

_____

What are three things you will try in the coming days to help your students succeed?

DATE: _____

What is your favorite part of being a teacher?

_____

_____

_____

_____

What was your biggest motivation today?

_____

_____

_____

_____

What was your biggest challenge today?

_____

_____

_____

_____

IT TAKES A BIG *heart* TO TEACH LITTLE *minds*

What are some successes you have seen lately?

What areas of growth have you seen
professionally? Personally?

DATE: _____

What topics are you most looking forward to teaching?

What topic have you been enjoying teaching lately?

_____

_____

_____

_____

_____

What topics are any of your students struggling with?
How can you help them?

_____

_____

_____

_____

_____

List four things you are proud of accomplishing with
your students recently?

Notes

STUDENT Spotlight

DATE: _____

It made me smile today when one of my
students said...

"

_____

_____

_____

_____

"

_____

A student who stood out was...

_____

_____

_____

_____

_____

A student that inspired me was...

_____

_____

_____

_____

_____

Who was struggling? Why?

_____

_____

_____

_____

A student made me laugh when...

_____

_____

_____

_____

WEEKLY *goals*

WEEK OF: _____

- _____
- _____
- _____
- _____
- _____
- _____
- _____
- _____

Things to note: _____

_____

*It's the teacher that makes the
difference, not the classroom.*
- MICHAEL MORPURGO

Lesson plan topics

They may forget what you said but they will not forget how you made them feel.
- CARL BUECHNER

Use this space to doodle,
brainstorm, journal or take notes

free your mind

Something I want to focus on as a teacher is...

_____

_____

_____

_____

_____

_____

How did you make learning fun for your
students this week:

- _____

- _____

- _____

- _____

- _____

TEACHING
reflections

Reflecting on your day including the highs and lows
is a great way to learn from your experiences

DATE: _____

What were the highlights of your day?

_____

_____

_____

_____

_____

_____

_____

_____

_____

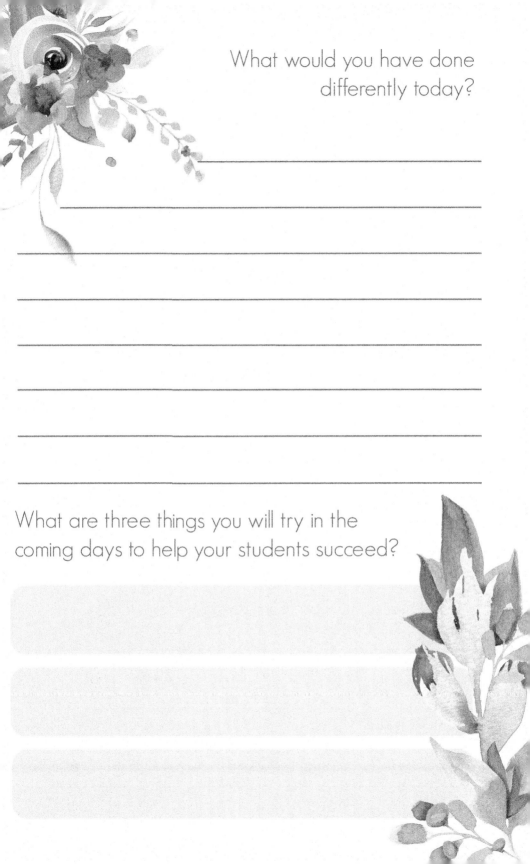

What would you have done
differently today?

_____

_____

_____

_____

_____

_____

_____

What are three things you will try in the
coming days to help your students succeed?

DATE: _____

What is your favorite part of being a teacher?

_____

_____

_____

_____

What was your biggest motivation today?

_____

_____

_____

_____

What was your biggest challenge today?

_____

_____

_____

_____

IT TAKES A BIG
heart
TO TEACH LITTLE
minds

What are some successes you have seen lately?

What areas of growth have you seen
professionally? Personally?

DATE: _____

What topics are you most looking forward to teaching?

What topic have you been enjoying teaching lately?

_____

_____

_____

_____

_____

_____

What topics are any of your students struggling with?
How can you help them?

_____

_____

_____

_____

_____

List four things you are proud of accomplishing with
your students recently?

Notes

STUDENT Spotlight

DATE: _____

It made me smile today when one of my
students said...

"

_____

_____

_____

_____

"

_____

A student who stood out was...

_____

_____

_____

_____

_____

A student that inspired me was...

_____

_____

_____

_____

_____

Who was struggling? Why?

_____

_____

_____

_____

A student made me laugh when...

_____

_____

_____

_____

WEEKLY *goals*

WEEK OF: _____

- _____
- _____
- _____
- _____
- _____
- _____
- _____
- _____
- _____

Things to note: _____

_____

*All students can learn and
succeed, but not in the same way
and not in the same day.*
- WILLIAM G. SPADY

Lesson plan topics

*I like a teacher who gives you something to take home
to think about besides homework.*
- LILY TOMLIN

Use this space to doodle,
brainstorm, journal or take notes

free your mind

Something I want to focus on as a teacher is...

_____

_____

_____

_____

_____

_____

How did you make learning fun for your
students this week:

- _____

- _____

- _____

- _____

- _____

TEACHING
reflections

Reflecting on your day including the highs and lows
is a great way to learn from your experiences

DATE: _____

What were the highlights of your day?

_____

_____

_____

_____

_____

_____

_____

_____

_____

What would you have done differently today?

_____

_____

_____

_____

_____

_____

_____

_____

What are three things you will try in the coming days to help your students succeed?

DATE: _____

What is your favorite part of being a teacher?

_____

_____

_____

_____

What was your biggest motivation today?

_____

_____

_____

_____

What was your biggest challenge today?

_____

_____

_____

_____

IT TAKES A BIG *heart* TO TEACH LITTLE *minds*

What are some successes you have seen lately?

What areas of growth have you seen professionally? Personally?

DATE: _____

What topics are you most looking forward to teaching?

What topic have you been enjoying teaching lately?

_____

_____

_____

_____

_____

_____

What topics are any of your students struggling with?
How can you help them?

_____

_____

_____

_____

_____

List four things you are proud of accomplishing with
your students recently?

Notes

STUDENT Spotlight

DATE: _____

It made me smile today when one of my
students said...

"
_____

_____

_____

_____

"
_____

A student who stood out was...

_____

_____

_____

_____

_____

A student that inspired me was...

_____

_____

_____

_____

_____

Who was struggling? Why?

_____

_____

_____

_____

A student made me laugh when...

_____

_____

_____

_____

WEEKLY *goals*

WEEK OF: _____

- _____
- _____
- _____
- _____
- _____
- _____
- _____
- _____
- _____

Things to note: _____

_____

Good teaching is one-fourth preparation and three-fourths theatre. **—GAIL GOODWIN**

Lesson plan topics

Use this space to doodle,
brainstorm, journal or take notes

free your mind

Something I want to focus on as a teacher is...

_____

_____

_____

_____

_____

How did you make learning fun for your
students this week:

- _____

- _____

- _____

- _____

- _____

TEACHING
reflections

Reflecting on your day including the highs and lows
is a great way to learn from your experiences

DATE: _____

What were the highlights of your day?

_____

_____

_____

_____

_____

_____

_____

_____

_____

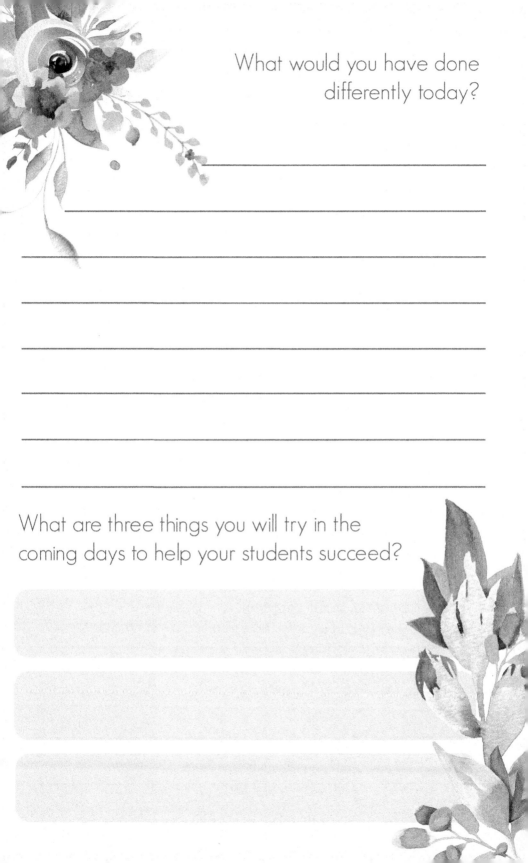

What would you have done
differently today?

_____

_____

_____

_____

_____

_____

_____

What are three things you will try in the
coming days to help your students succeed?

DATE: _____

What is your favorite part of being a teacher?

_____

_____

_____

_____

What was your biggest motivation today?

_____

_____

_____

_____

What was your biggest challenge today?

_____

_____

_____

_____

IT TAKES A BIG *heart* TO TEACH LITTLE *minds*

What are some successes you have seen lately?

What areas of growth have you seen professionally? Personally?

What topics are you most looking forward to teaching?

What topic have you been enjoying teaching lately?

_____

_____

_____

_____

_____

What topics are any of your students struggling with?
How can you help them?

_____

_____

_____

_____

_____

_____

List four things you are proud of accomplishing with
your students recently?

Notes

_____

_____

_____

_____

_____

_____

_____

_____

_____

_____

_____

_____

_____

STUDENT Spotlight

DATE: _____

It made me smile today when one of my
students said...

"

_____

_____

_____

_____

"

_____

A student who stood out was...

_____

_____

_____

_____

_____

A student that inspired me was...

_____

_____

_____

_____

_____

Who was struggling? Why?

_____

_____

_____

_____

A student made me laugh when...

_____

_____

_____

_____

_____

WEEKLY *goals*

WEEK OF: _____

- _____
  _____
- _____
  _____
- _____
  _____
- _____
  _____
- _____
  _____
- _____
  _____
- _____
  _____
- _____
  _____

Things to note: _____

_____

I touch the future. I teach.
- CHRISTA MCAULIFFE

Lesson plan topics

The task of the modern educator is not to cut down jungles, but to irrigate deserts.
- C. S. LEWIS

Use this space to doodle,
brainstorm, journal or take notes
free your mind

Something I want to focus on as a teacher is...

_____

_____

_____

_____

_____

How did you make learning fun for your
students this week:

- _____

- _____

- _____

- _____

- _____

TEACHING
reflections

Reflecting on your day including the highs and lows
is a great way to learn from your experiences

DATE: _____

What were the highlights of your day?

_____

_____

_____

_____

_____

_____

_____

_____

_____

What would you have done
differently today?

_____

_____

_____

_____

_____

_____

_____

_____

What are three things you will try in the
coming days to help your students succeed?

DATE: _____

What is your favorite part of being a teacher?

_____

_____

_____

_____

What was your biggest motivation today?

_____

_____

_____

_____

What was your biggest challenge today?

_____

_____

_____

_____

IT TAKES A BIG *heart* TO TEACH LITTLE *minds*

What are some successes you have seen lately?

What areas of growth have you seen
professionally? Personally?

DATE: _____

What topics are you most looking forward to teaching?

What topic have you been enjoying teaching lately?

_____

_____

_____

_____

_____

What topics are any of your students struggling with?
How can you help them?

_____

_____

_____

_____

_____

_____

List four things you are proud of accomplishing with
your students recently?

Notes

STUDENT Spotlight

DATE: _____

It made me smile today when one of my
students said...

"

_____

_____

_____

_____

"

_____

A student who stood out was...

_____

_____

_____

_____

A student that inspired me was...

_____

_____

_____

_____

_____

Who was struggling? Why?

_____

_____

_____

_____

A student made me laugh when...

_____

_____

_____

_____

_____

WEEKLY *goals*

WEEK OF: _____

- _____
  _____
- _____
  _____
- _____
  _____
- _____
  _____
- _____
  _____
- _____
  _____
- _____
  _____
- _____
  _____
- _____

Things to note: _____

_____

If you have to put someone on a pedestal, put teachers. They are society's heroes. – GUY KAWASAKI

Lesson plan topics

The duties of a teacher are neither few nor small, but they elevate the mind and give energy to the character. — DORTHEA DIX

Use this space to doodle,
brainstorm, journal or take notes
free your mind

Something I want to focus on as a teacher is...

_____

_____

_____

_____

_____

_____

How did you make learning fun for your
students this week:

- _____

- _____

- _____

- _____

- _____

TEACHING
reflections

Reflecting on your day including the highs and lows
is a great way to learn from your experiences

DATE: _____

What were the highlights of your day?

_____

_____

_____

_____

_____

_____

_____

_____

What would you have done differently today?

_____

_____

_____

_____

_____

_____

_____

_____

What are three things you will try in the coming days to help your students succeed?

DATE: _____

What is your favorite part of being a teacher?

_____

_____

_____

_____

What was your biggest motivation today?

_____

_____

_____

_____

What was your biggest challenge today?

_____

_____

_____

_____

IT TAKES A BIG *heart* TO TEACH LITTLE *minds*

What are some successes you have seen lately?

What areas of growth have you seen professionally? Personally?

DATE: _____

What topics are you most looking forward to teaching?

What topic have you been enjoying teaching lately?

_____

_____

_____

_____

_____

_____

What topics are any of your students struggling with? How can you help them?

_____

_____

_____

_____

_____

List four things you are proud of accomplishing with your students recently?

Notes

_____

_____

_____

_____

_____

_____

_____

_____

_____

_____

_____

_____

STUDENT Spotlight

DATE: _____

It made me smile today when one of my
students said...

"

_____

_____

_____

_____

"

_____

A student who stood out was...

_____

_____

_____

_____

_____

A student that inspired me was...

_____

_____

_____

_____

_____

Who was struggling? Why?

_____

_____

_____

_____

A student made me laugh when...

_____

_____

_____

_____

WEEKLY *goals*

WEEK OF: _____

- _____
- _____
- _____
- _____
- _____
- _____
- _____
- _____
- _____

Things to note: _____

_____

To this end, the greatest asset of a school is the personality of the teacher. — JOHN STRACHAN

Lesson plan topics

The whole purpose of education is to turn mirrors
into windows.
- SYDNEY J. HARRIS

Use this space to doodle,
brainstorm, journal or take notes
free your mind

Something I want to focus on as a teacher is...

_____

_____

_____

_____

_____

_____

How did you make learning fun for your students this week:

- _____

- _____

- _____

- _____

- _____

TEACHING
reflections

Reflecting on your day including the highs and lows
is a great way to learn from your experiences

DATE: _____

What were the highlights of your day?

_____

_____

_____

_____

_____

_____

_____

_____

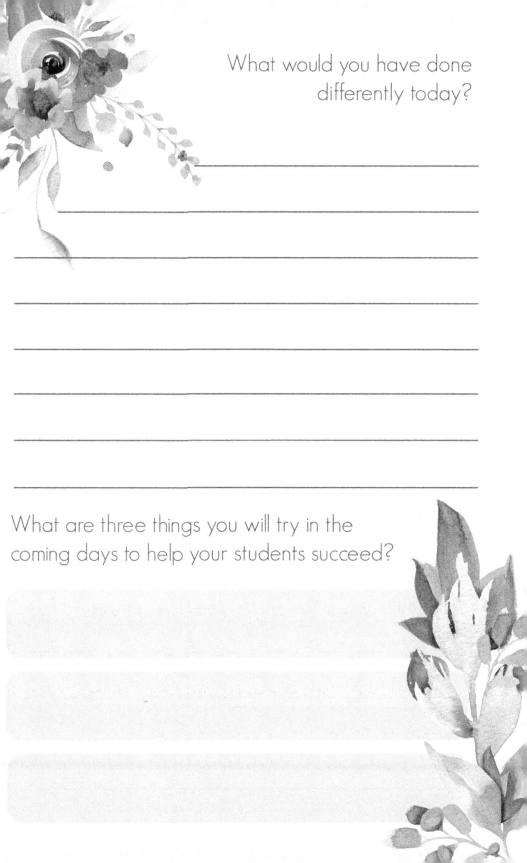

What would you have done differently today?

_____

_____

_____

_____

_____

_____

_____

What are three things you will try in the coming days to help your students succeed?

DATE: _____

What is your favorite part of being a teacher?

_____

_____

_____

_____

What was your biggest motivation today?

_____

_____

_____

_____

What was your biggest challenge today?

_____

_____

_____

_____

IT TAKES A BIG *heart* TO TEACH LITTLE *minds*

What are some successes you have seen lately?

What areas of growth have you seen professionally? Personally?

DATE: _____

What topics are you most looking forward to teaching?

What topic have you been enjoying teaching lately?

_____

_____

_____

_____

_____

What topics are any of your students struggling with?
How can you help them?

_____

_____

_____

_____

_____

List four things you are proud of accomplishing with
your students recently?

Notes

STUDENT Spotlight

DATE: _____

It made me smile today when one of my
students said...

"
_____
_____
_____
_____
"
_____

A student who stood out was...

_____
_____
_____
_____
_____

A student that inspired me was...

_____

_____

_____

_____

_____

Who was struggling? Why?

_____

_____

_____

A student made me laugh when...

_____

_____

_____

_____

WEEKLY *goals*

WEEK OF: _____

- _____
- _____
- _____
- _____
- _____
- _____
- _____
- _____

Things to note: _____

_____

What sculpture is to a block of marble, education is to a human soul. - JOSEPH ADDISON

Lesson plan topics

Education breeds confidence. Confidence breeds hope.
Hope breeds peace.
— CONFUCIUS

Use this space to doodle,
brainstorm, journal or take notes

free your mind

Something I want to focus on as a teacher is...

_____

_____

_____

_____

_____

How did you make learning fun for your
students this week:

- _____

- _____

- _____

- _____

- _____

TEACHING reflections

Reflecting on your day including the highs and lows
is a great way to learn from your experiences

DATE: _____

What were the highlights of your day?

_____

_____

_____

_____

_____

_____

_____

_____

_____

What would you have done
differently today?

_____

_____

_____

_____

_____

_____

_____

_____

What are three things you will try in the
coming days to help your students succeed?

DATE: _____

What is your favorite part of being a teacher?

_____

_____

_____

_____

What was your biggest motivation today?

_____

_____

_____

_____

What was your biggest challenge today?

_____

_____

_____

_____

IT TAKES A BIG *heart* TO TEACH LITTLE *minds*

What are some successes you have seen lately?

What areas of growth have you seen
professionally? Personally?

DATE: _____

What topics are you most looking forward to teaching?

What topic have you been enjoying teaching lately?

_____

_____

_____

_____

_____

What topics are any of your students struggling with?
How can you help them?

_____

_____

_____

_____

_____

List four things you are proud of accomplishing with
your students recently?

Notes

STUDENT Spotlight

DATE: _____

It made me smile today when one of my
students said...

"

_____

_____

_____

_____

"

_____

A student who stood out was...

_____

_____

_____

_____

_____

A student that inspired me was...

_____

_____

_____

_____

_____

Who was struggling? Why?

_____

_____

_____

_____

A student made me laugh when...

_____

_____

_____

_____

WEEKLY *goals*

WEEK OF: _____

- _____
- _____
- _____
- _____
- _____
- _____
- _____
- _____
- _____

Things to note: _____

_____

Teachers can change lives with just the right mix of chalk and challenges. - JOYCE MEYER

Lesson plan topics

Better than a thousand days of diligent study is one
day with a great teacher.
- JAPANESE PROVERB

Use this space to doodle,
brainstorm, journal or take notes
free your mind

Something I want to focus on as a teacher is...

_____

_____

_____

_____

_____

_____

How did you make learning fun for your
students this week:

- _____

- _____

- _____

- _____

- _____

TEACHING
reflections

Reflecting on your day including the highs and lows is a great way to learn from your experiences

DATE: _____

What were the highlights of your day?

_____

_____

_____

_____

_____

_____

_____

_____

What would you have done
differently today?

_____

_____

_____

_____

_____

_____

_____

What are three things you will try in the
coming days to help your students succeed?

DATE: _____

What is your favorite part of being a teacher?

_____

_____

_____

_____

What was your biggest motivation today?

_____

_____

_____

_____

What was your biggest challenge today?

_____

_____

_____

_____

IT TAKES A BIG *heart* TO TEACH LITTLE *minds*

What are some successes you have seen lately?

What areas of growth have you seen
professionally? Personally?

DATE: _____

What topics are you most looking forward to teaching?

What topic have you been enjoying teaching lately?

_____

_____

_____

_____

_____

What topics are any of your students struggling with?
How can you help them?

_____

_____

_____

_____

_____

_____

List four things you are proud of accomplishing with
your students recently?

Notes

STUDENT Spotlight

DATE: _____

It made me smile today when one of my
students said...

"

_____

_____

_____

_____
"

_____

A student who stood out was...

_____

_____

_____

_____

_____

A student that inspired me was...

_____

_____

_____

_____

_____

Who was struggling? Why?

_____

_____

_____

_____

A student made me laugh when...

_____

_____

_____

_____

WEEKLY *goals*

WEEK OF: _____

- _____
- _____
- _____
- _____
- _____
- _____
- _____
- _____
- _____

Things to note: _____

_____

What a teacher is, is more
important than what he teaches
-KARL MENNINGER

Lesson plan topics

Teachers affect eternity; no one can tell where their influence stops.
- HENRY BROOKS ADAM

Use this space to doodle,
brainstorm, journal or take notes
free your mind

Something I want to focus on as a teacher is...

_____

_____

_____

_____

_____

_____

How did you make learning fun for your students this week:

- _____

- _____

- _____

- _____

- _____

TEACHING
reflections

Reflecting on your day including the highs and lows
is a great way to learn from your experiences

DATE: _____

What were the highlights of your day?

_____

_____

_____

_____

_____

_____

_____

_____

_____

What would you have done
differently today?

_____

_____

_____

_____

_____

_____

_____

What are three things you will try in the
coming days to help your students succeed?

DATE: _____

What is your favorite part of being a teacher?

_____

_____

_____

_____

What was your biggest motivation today?

_____

_____

_____

_____

What was your biggest challenge today?

_____

_____

_____

_____

IT TAKES A BIG *heart* TO TEACH LITTLE *minds*

What are some successes you have seen lately?

What areas of growth have you seen professionally? Personally?

DATE: _____

What topics are you most looking forward to teaching?

What topic have you been enjoying teaching lately?

_____

_____

_____

_____

_____

_____

What topics are any of your students struggling with?
How can you help them?

_____

_____

_____

_____

_____

_____

List four things you are proud of accomplishing with
your students recently?

Notes

_____

_____

_____

_____

_____

_____

_____

_____

_____

_____

_____

_____

_____

Notes

_____

_____

_____

_____

_____

_____

_____

_____

_____

_____

_____

_____

Made in the USA
Columbia, SC
31 August 2020